Rat-a-Tat, Pitter Pat

Sounds by Alan Benjamin
Pictures by Margaret Miller

Thomas Y. Crowell   New York

Rat-a-Tat, Pitter Pat
Text copyright © 1987 by Alan Benjamin
Photographs copyright © 1987 by Margaret Miller
Printed in the U.S.A. All rights reserved.
Typography by Albert Cetta

Library of Congress Cataloging-in-Publication Data
Benjamin, Alan.
   Rat-a-tat, pitter pat.

   Summary: Black and white photographs illustrate rhyming sounds such as "sizzle/drizzle," "pop/plop," and "slurp/burp."
   1. English language—Onomatopoeic words—Juvenile literature.   [1. English language—Onomatopoeic words.   2. Sounds, Words for.   3. Vocabulary]   I. Miller, Margaret, 1945-   , ill.   II. Title.
PE1597.B46   1987   428.1   87-568
ISBN 0-690-04609-X
ISBN 0-690-04611-1 lib. bdg.

1 2 3 4 5 6 7 8 9 10
First Edition

For Jessica
—A. B.

For my mother and father
—M. M.

knock knock

tick tock

sizzle

drizzle

cheep cheep

beep beep

clap

tap

snap

bow wow

meow

pluck

muck

whack

quack

munch

crunch

hush

gush

pop

plop

ding dong

ping pong

choo choo

moo

splash

crash

purr

whirr

rip

snip

zip

drip

slurp

burp

rat-a-tat   pitter pat

splat

Margaret Miller

Alan Benjamin

click